Once There Was a Hassid

retold by: Devorah Omer

drawings: Aaron Shevo

Adama Books, New York

No part of this publication may be reproduced, stored in a
retrieval system, or transmitted in any form or by any means,
electronic, mechanical, photocopying, recording
or otherwise (brief quotations used in magazines or newspaper
reviews excepted), without the prior permission of the publisher.

translated by: Edward Levin
production: Ruth Eilat

Computerized typography: M. Rachlin Printing Ltd.

© Modan Publishing House Ltd

ISBN 0-915361-73-6
Adama Books, 306 West 38th Street, New York, N.Y. 10018

Printed in Israel

The Birth of the Baal Shem Tov

There once was a Jew named Rabbi Eliezer who lived in Poland. He was a goodhearted person. He was pious and wise, and knew the entire Torah. Rabbi Eliezer had a small shop in the marketplace, in which he sold bread, salted fish, and onions to people who walked through the marketplace.

Very few customers came to Rabbi Eliezer's small shop. Unlike the other shopkeepers, he did not stand at the entrance to his shop and call out to the passsersby, to persuade them to come into the shop and buy. It was Rabbi Eliezer's custom to sit in his shop, by the small window, and look outside, at the sun, the sky, the trees covered with green leaves, and at the flowers which were in bloom.

Rabbi Eliezer did not earn a lot, but his earnings were enough to buy bread, salted fish, and tea for himself and his wife. Rabbi Eliezer needed no more than this. He and his wife were happy, and they were content with their lot. They lacked only one thing – a son. Rabbi Eliezer prayed, and asked of God:

"Master of the Universe! Please, give me a son, who will be good and wise, who will teach people what is good and what is bad."

Rabbi Eliezer's prayer reached Heaven. The angel Gabriel heard his prayer, and immediately sent forth his hand to the Palace of Light. There, in the Palace of Light, were the souls of all the children who had not yet been born. The angel Gabriel took one soul, which was shining and glittering like the light of the Seven Days of Creation. The angel Gabriel wanted to dress this soul in the body of an infant and send it to Rabbi Eliezer, so that he would have the son for whom he had asked. The ministering angels saw this and were exceedingly glad. The angels said, "You have chosen a brilliant soul. Rabbi Eliezer's son will be known for his wisdom."

All of a sudden, the skies darkened and were covered with black clouds. Satan had risen to heaven. He had come from Below all the way to Heaven, and he began to shout.

All the angels were amazed: "Why do you refuse to have Rabbi Eliezer's prayer answered?

He is a *tzaddik*, a holy man, and his request must be fulfilled!"

"**He is a holy man?**" Satan let out a mighty laugh. "In what is he so holy?"

"He is an honest man," the angels answered. "He does not cheat, and he does not lie."

"It is not because he is such a holy man that Rabbi Eliezer does not lie," Satan said. "He is a simple, innocent person who does not know how to lie. Just teach him, and he will do that."

"He is not like the other merchants," the angels said, "Rabbi Eliezer isn't interested just in making money. He makes do with what he has, and even shares this with others."

"This is not because he's such a holy man," Satan declared. "He simply doesn't know what money and possessions are, since he never had any money. If he gets a taste of wealth, he'll soon change his tune."

"Rabbi Eliezer observes all the commandments," the angels said, "he observes them all strictly."

"He lives among Jews," Satan said, "let's see if he would keep the commandments if he were to live among non-Jews."

The angels heard Satan's words. They covered their faces with their wings, and did not know what to reply to him.

The angel Gabriel returned the glowing soul to the Palace of Light in Heaven, and no son was born to Rabbi Eliezer and his wife for many years. The two were sad and lonely. They saw that evil, theft, and envy were rampant, and they did not have a son who would grow up and teach his fellow humans wisdom and knowledge.

Rabbi Eliezer and his wife left their home and set out for the forest. Rabbi Eliezer built a small hut from the branches of trees, he drank water from the river, ate the fruits of the trees, and spent the entire day praying. But a son was not born to him because Satan, the Adversary, would not permit this.

And then one day, robbers fell upon Rabbi Eliezer's hut. They searched in the hut for gold and silver, but found nothing, because Rabbi Eliezer had no possessions at all.

The robbers were about to kill Rabbi Eliezer and his wife. Rabbi Eliezer looked at the chief of the robbers with his warm, shining eyes – and suddenly the robber turned into another person, and his evil heart was filled with goodness.

"Do not kill the man and his wife!" the chief of the robbers commanded his men.

The robbers were extremely surprised, because their chief never took pity on anyone. The robber chieftain was afraid that his own men would kill him, because he had taken pity on this man. He told them, "We haven't found anything here, and we won't find anything if we kill the man. It will be worth our while to sell him as a slave, for money." The robbers heard their chief's words and said, "You have spoken wisely." They immediately freed Rabbi Eliezer's wife and took the husband with them.

They brought him to the slave market and announced loudly, "A great sage for sale! Who wants to buy a sage?"

The viceroy of the king, who happened to be passing through the marketplace, heard this announcement. He looked in Rabbi Eliezer's face, and what did he see? Eyes shining like stars, and a face beaming with the light of wisdom. The viceroy bought Rabbi Eliezer and brought him to his home.

And then – as soon as Rabbi Eliezer entered the viceroy's home, the entire house was filled with light. The viceroy went out with him to the garden, and the trees dropped their fruit and flowers at his feet. The birds sang more beautifully than he had ever heard. The viceroy knew then that the slave he had purchased was not like other men, and he appointed Rabbi Eliezer over all his other slaves and servants. He gave him a fine room, and the best food and clothing to be had. But Rabbi Eliezer ate nothing and drank nothing from the table of this official. He studied Torah during his every free moment, and he ate only seeds and drank only water from the well. Rabbi Eliezer was very careful to observe all of the Lord's commandments.

One day the viceroy came into his house in a sad mood. 'What is the matter, my exalted master?" Rabbi Eliezer asked him. "Great trouble has descended upon me," the viceroy told him. "The king whom I counsel waged war upon all his enemies, and defeated them all. Only one fortress remains, surrounded by water on all sides. Every ship which attempts to approach the fortress capsizes and cannot reach the shore. Today the king has commanded me to find a way to conquer the fortress. If I do not give him good advice by tomorrow morning, the king will depose me from my high position."

Rabbi Eliezer heard the viceroy's words, thought for a while, and said: "Tell the king that the enemy has encircled the fortress with strong pronged bars of iron, concealed underneath the water. If these bars will be cut, the ships will be able to approach the shore and conquer the fortress."

The viceroy heard this, and hurried to the palace to reveal to the king the secret why the ships all capsized when they neared the fortress. "If we cut these bars we will be able to conquer the fortress," the king's advisor stated in a decisive tone.

"And who told this to you?" the king asked, amazed. The viceroy told him about the slave he had bought, telling him that the man was exceedingly wise.

The king ordered that Rabbi Eliezer be brought to the palace. As soon as he entered the palace, it was filled with a great light. The king knew then that the man was indeed a great sage, and that his words could be relied upon.

The king immediately ordered that all the ships be made ready. Rabbi Eliezer boarded the first ship and they set sail for the fortress. All the birds left their tree branches, flew above Rabbi Eliezer's ship, and sang songs of praise and victory throughout the entire voyage. The ships approached the fortress. The birds suddenly ceased their singing. "Stop!" Rabbi Eliezer ordered. We must not sail any further, lest we capsize!"

The sailors stopped the ships. They took large, strong shears, reached into the water, and – as Rabbi Eliezer had said – they found strong, piercing metal bars under the water. They cut the bars and the birds began singing once again.

"Now we may proceed without fear," Rabbi Eliezer said. The ships sailed toward the fortress, and none of them capsized or were damaged. The soldiers stormed the fortress and took it without difficulty. Then the king removed his ring from his finger, gave it to Rabbi Eliezer, and said to him, "You shall be as my son, you shall live in my palace, what is mine is yours, and I shall even give you my daughter as a wife."

Rabbi Eliezer did not desire the king's daughter, because he remembered his own wife and missed her greatly. Rabbi Eliezer bowed down before the king and said, "My lord, who am I that I should marry your daughter?"

"You are wise and discerning," said the king, "you are worthy to be the son-in-law of the king."

"One miracle was performed for me with God's help," Rabbi Eliezer said. "If an additional miracle will also be performed for me and I conquer a second fortress, then perhaps I will be worthy to sit in your palace."

All the people around them heard this and were greatly amazed. Such a thing had never been heard before – that the king offered his daughter as a wife to someone, and the person refused.

The king heard Rabbi Eliezer's words, and realized that a truly unique person was before him. He did everything that Rabbi Eliezer asked of him.

Rabbi Eliezer boarded a ship and sailed on the sea by himself. Entire flocks of birds flew above him and sang for him. The boat sailed on for seven days and seven nights, until it reached the shore. Rabbi Eliezer went down from the ship, accompanied by the birds which continued to sing for him.

Rabbi Eliezer walked for seven days and seven nights, with the ever-present birds showing him the way. He finally came to a small village. The birds flew toward a small, run-down house, which stood at the edge of the village. They flocked around the house, singing merrily.

Rabbi Eliezer approached the house, opened the door – and there in the house was his wife, sitting and reading from the prayerbook!

Rabbi Eliezer was exceedingly happy to find his wife, whom he had not seen for many years. His wife was even happier, for she had not known whether her husband was alive or dead.

Rabbi Eliezer did not return to the palace of the king. He was happy in the little, run-down house, with his wife whom he loved. He gladly renounced all the king's bounty. He drank from the water of the stream and ate from the fruits of the trees. He looked at the trees and flowers all around him, and he enjoyed the sun and the skies. Only one thing was missing to make his happiness complete – a son.

Rabbi Eliezer greatly desired a son, and prayed to God again and again. His prayer ascended to Heaven. The angel Gabriel heard his prayer, and sent forth his hand to the

Palace of Light in Heaven and lifted out one soul which was all radiance. He wanted to dress it in the body of an infant and send it to Rabbi Eliezer, so that he would have a son. Then the skies darkened and were covered with blacker than black clouds. Satan had risen to heaven. He had come from Below, and he began to shout: "No! I will not allow it!"

The ministering angels said to Satan: "Now you can no longer claim anything against Rabbi Eliezer. He could have become wealthy, but he did not want riches. He kept the commandments all the time he lived among the non-Jews. His prayer deserves to be heard!" Satan could raise no further objections. The angel Gabriel took the great, shining soul, dressed it in the body of an infant, and brought it down into the world.

And when the time came, a son was born to Rabbi Eliezer, and he called him Israel.

The boy grew up and became great in Torah, and he was called Israel Baal Shem Tov.

The Story of the Sorcerer Valkilak

When Rabbi Israel Baal Shem Tov was a little boy, his father and mother died and he became an orphan. Generous people cared for him so that he could study Torah. The child studied in a *heder*, a little one-room school. Only a few days passed, and he already knew how to read and write, and continued to be an excellent pupil.

But the study of the Torah was not enough. A person must have bread to eat and clothes to wear. Israel did not want charity from other people; he wanted to support himself. The boy searched for a trade at which he could work in the early morning hours, before he went to study in the *heder*, and afterwards at night, after he was through studying for the day. He searched and he found what he was looking for.

Every day Israel would wake up early, while it was still dark outside. He went to all the houses, collected all the little children, and brought them to the schoolroom to study Torah. And when they finished studying, as the sun was beginning to go down, Israel came and brought each child back to his home.

Israel walked at the head of all the children, and sang in a very pleasant voice. The children joined in his singing, and the entire village rang with their song. The birds awakened and began to chirp and sing together with Israel and the children. The sun rose and also joined the singing. The trees waved their leaves and sang too. The flowers opened their colorful petals and joined the song. All the animals and insects added their voices as well, and even the stones in the fields and the walls of the buildings began to sing.

This song went up and up to Heaven, and all the heavenly spheres were filled with joy and song. The ministering angels rejoiced, and they too joined this song.

Only Satan and his evil agents did not sing and did not rejoice. They were sad and angry, because Satan and the demons hated singing and joy. Because, you see, where there is joy and song, Satan cannot enter. He is powerful only in a place of sadness and weeping. And now the children were singing every morning and every evening, and the melody spread throughout the entire world and went up to Heaven.

There was a tremendous commotion in Sheol, the land of Satan and his agents. The demons flew around and waved their black wings, they flew around and shrieked bitterly, "What will we do, Master Satan? What will happen to us? Can't you, Satan, king of the demons, stop this singing?"

Satan answered the demons, saying, "I will think on this matter."

"Do it now, immediately!" all the demons pressed their king. "Can't you fight this little Jewish boy, Israel?"

"Of course I am powerful enough to do this!" Satan said.

Satan immediately used his magical powers and turned himself into a sorcerer by the name of Valkilak. This sorcerer was terrible to look at: he had tiny, evil eyes, a large, crooked nose, and a gaping mouth with huge, sharp teeth sticking out of it. This sorcerer had the black wings of a bat, the body of a human being, and the feet of a chicken, with long, sharp nails.

Satan, in the form of the sorcerer, came down to the main street of the city and waited in hiding, in a corner. It was late at night. In a little while the sun would rise, and then....

Not much time passed, and the young Israel appeared, coming out of a small, run-down house. His face still looked sleepy, but he strode out into the street. And – what a wonder – just as soon as Israel left his house, he began to sing his melody, and the night was no longer so black and gloomy. The birds began to sing. The sun sent forth its first rays. Israel went from house to house, collecting the small children. And Satan, in the form of Valkilak the sorcerer, waited in the corner. The song and the melody pouring forth from the mouths of the children was just terrible to Satan's ears. And when the children were joined in their singing by the birds, the animals, the trees, and the flowers, Satan could not bear it any longer. "Away with you!" Satan called in a loud voice, and ran after the children who were following Israel.

The children saw the horrible sorcerer, and were terribly frightened. They ran as fast as they could, all the way back to their homes. "There's a terrible sorcerer outside!" the children cried out. They refused to go to study Torah, because they were afraid to leave their homes and go out into the street. "There's a sorcerer standing outside!" they said. "He has the wings of a bat and the feet of a chicken, his nose is crooked, and his teeth are long and sharp."

Not a single child went to learn Torah that day. The melody was not heard in the streets of

the city. Everyone was sad. All singing had stopped in the land, and there was sadness even in heaven. Only Satan and his demons rejoiced and danced in Sheol. They shouted and cried out for joy.

One day passed. Two days passed. The children still did not dare to go outside their houses, for fear of the terrible sorcerer. The entire world was filled with sadness.

Young Israel thought to himself, "What will I do?" He thought and thought, and he remembered what his father had told him before he died: "Remember, my son, do not be afraid of anything, because God is with you, and He will help you."

"I don't have to be afraid. The children cannot hide in their homes and not come out to study Torah," he said to himself. "It's very bad that there is no longer any singing in the world."

Israel took a big, heavy stick in his hand and went to the houses of the children. In every house he asked that they send the children with him the next day. He promised them that he would bring the children safely to the *heder*, and that nothing bad would happen to them on the way. Israel encouraged all the children. He cheered them up, so that they would not be afraid of the sorcerer. "Look at the big stick in my hand!" he told them. "I will beat the sorcerer if he comes again."

The children saw the big stick in Israel's hand and they were no longer afraid.

The parents remembered the miracles that God had performed for Rabbi Eliezer, Israel's father. They also knew that it was not good that their children were not studying Torah. They remembered the singing and the melody that filled the world when the children went out to the *heder*. They agreed to give their children to Israel, so that he could take them early in the morning to study Torah.

All that night fear stirred in the hearts of many people in the city. Would Israel succeed in beating the sorcerer? Would Valkilak harm the children? And all that night Israel prepared himself. Early in the morning he left his house, his big stick in his hand, and began walking throughout the city from house to house, collecting the children.

Israel marched at the head of the children, and sang in his beautiful voice. The children joined his singing. There was no longer any fear in their hearts. The wonderful melody was heard throughout the world once again. The birds arose from their slumber and began to chirp together with the children. The sun hurried to send its first rays, and it also joined the song. The flowers opened their petals, the trees moved their leaves, the animals and the birds joined in. They all began to sing together with Israel and the children. The world was filled with happiness and song, and the joyous song rose up and up, to Heaven, and all the Heavenly spheres were filled with rejoicing.

The demons heard this and were filled with anger. "What is this? Are they singing once again on earth?" they called out to Satan.

"They will stop singing immediately!" Satan said. He again turned himself into the sorcerer Valkilak. Satan flapped his black bat wings, and quickly went down to the main street of the city. He hid in the corner and waited until Israel would come to collect the children and return them to their homes. "I'll fall on them and I'll scare them so badly," he thought to his evil self, "that they'll never, ever, dare to come out of their houses and study Torah!"

Night fell. It was dark outside. Israel, who had been busy studying all day, was about to go outside to return the children to their homes.

He took his big stick in his hand and walked through the street, with the children following him.

Israel began to sing, and the children sang with him. The moon shone. The stars twinkled and joined the singing. The birds, the trees, the flowers, all sang with them. The entire world sang with them. Satan, in the form of the evil sorcerer, hid in the corner and waited. When the children drew near, the sorcerer came out of his hiding place, ran with his chicken feet, flapped his wings, and cried out in a deafening voice, "Away with you! Be scared!"

The children were very frightened. But Israel was not frightened or alarmed. He raised his big stick and struck the sorcerer a mighty blow on the head.

The sorcerer fell to the ground and did not rise again. Israel and all the children went safely on their way. They all sang loudly.

From then on Israel continued to take the children every morning, and to bring them back to their homes in the evening. And Israel and the children with him continued to sing in a mighty voice. And the ministering angels and all God's creatures sang with them. And Satan and the evil demons never again dared to interfere with the singing, the song of Torah and light.

The Horse Who Brought a Treasure

There was once in a small village in Poland a very poor Jew, who was a holy and very goodhearted person. He was a simple person, a coachman. He had a thin, weak, horse and a broken carriage in which he drove people to the marketplace and back. Not many people were willing to travel in this rickety carriage, harnessed to an old horse. The coachman earned a very meager living.

But he made do with what he had. He was happy with his lot, and never asked for more than what he earned. Every Thursday he would get up very early and work until the afternoon. Then he would bring all the money he had earned that day to his wife. His wife used this money to buy candles for the Sabbath, wine for *kiddush*, and if there was enough money, even meat, fish, and *hallot*, the special Sabbath loaves. The coachman never went out to work on Fridays. "The horse needs his rest, and I need the Torah," he said. The horse would stand in the stable and eat straw, while the coachman would go to the ritual bath, to immerse himself in honor of the Sabbath. Then he would go to the synagogue and sit there until the Sabbath entered.

This was the coachman's custom, week after week.

And then, one night – it was on a Thursday night, after midnight – a thief entered the courtyard of the coachman's house. He silently opened the door to the little stable and took the horse out. The thief even stole the carriage which stood in the courtyard. No one in the house heard anything.

The coachman got out of bed especially early, as was his custom every Thursday. He went outside to harness the horse to the wagon – and he found the stable empty. The horse was gone. Even the carriage had vanished. The coachman was extremely distressed by this. But what could he do? He went back inside the house, sat down by the oven, and began to study Torah. The rest of the family woke up, totally amazed. Why was Father sitting in the house on Thursday morning, instead of going out to work? The coachman told them what had happened. His wife started to weep. The children also began to cry bitterly. Everyone knew that without the horse and wagon they would not even have the bread and onions they ate all week long. And how would they buy food for the Sabbath, which was fast approaching?

The coachman and his wife knew that they had only two choices: either to go hungry, or to ask for charity to buy food for the Sabbath.

The coachman said to his wife, "The Holy One, blessed be He, commanded us to honor the Sabbath with food, with wine, and with candles. But if He does not want this to be so this Sabbath, we will honor His will."

"That's not so," his wife argued with him, "perhaps the Holy One, blessed be He, desires that people will give us charity, so that they will be able to perform a good deed?"

But the coachman would not agree to beg.

"I never asked for anything from others," he declared, "and I will not do so this time, either."

"May it be as you wish," his wife sighed.

"I want you to promise me," the coachman said to his wife, "that when I go to the ritual bath and the synagogue on Friday, that you will not tell a soul that we do not have any money for the Sabbath, so that they will not entreat us to accept charity from them. I do not want this. Promise me that you will not take anything from anybody."

His wife promised him, and the coachman was relieved. He sat next to the oven and sang, as if he was not at all distressed about what had befallen them, and the fate that awaited them without a horse and wagon. The opposite was true. He looked as if he was happy for having an extra day to sing songs from the prayerbook and to study Torah.

And this was not all. His wife and the children listened to the sound of his prayers, and a great weight was lifted off their troubled hearts. They did not feel any hunger or suffering. They sat in a circle around the coachman and listened to his studying and prayers the entire day.

At the same time the thief was making his way to the forest. It was the middle of winter, and the air was frosty. The thief decided to go to the forest to cut wood. Then he would load the wood on the wagon, bring it to the city, and sell it for a lot of money.

The thief, riding in the wagon, came to the forest he searched for, and found a tall, thick tree. He raised his axe and began chopping away at the trunk of the tree. At first, his blows only made a small crack in the thick trunk. Then the thief struck another blow. He saw something sparkling inside the tree.

He bent down to look – and he saw a treasure in gold coins concealed within the hollow tree trunk. The thief was exceedingly happy at this sight. He began to remove the coins and put them in a big sack. There were many coins there. The thief continued to chop away at the tree, in order to enlarge the hole, so that he could put both his hands into the tree trunk and take out the coins. He continued chopping away at the trunk, until the tree began to tilt and almost fell over. The thief stuck his hands into the hollow trunk and took out more and more coins. When the sack was full, he took a second sack and filled this one as well with gold coins, because the tree really contained an enormous treasure.

The thief loaded the sacks, which were filled with the gold coins, on the wagon. The thief didn't care whether the heavy load was too much for the old and weak horse. He covered the sacks with branches, so that no one would see what was inside the wagon, and began to urge the horse on. The horse went along slowly, because the load was heavy and the horse was old and feeble. The thief raised his whip and struck the horse again and again, until it started bleeding. "Giddap! Faster!" But the horse walked slowly, because it could go no faster.

And then, when the thief began to leave the forest, a new thought popped into his head. "Maybe a few coins fell next to the tree without my noticing them?" He immediately decided to return to the forest and search on the ground, among the weeds and plants. He might find another coin or two there. The enormous treasure that he had found was not enough for him. He wanted more and more. The thief began to whip the poor horse. He turned the wagon around and made his way back to the forest.

When he came back to the same place, he began to feel around on the ground, hoping to find another coin or two. And then, as he was searching among the branches of the tree which was leaning over dangerously – the tree suddenly fell over, snapped off from the trunk with a trmendous Crack! and fell on the thief! The thief was trapped between the branches and could not get free. The branches held him tightly, and prevented him even from moving.

The thief began to cry in a loud voice for help. But this was deep in the forest, in a spot where no one would pass by. No one heard his voice, and no one came to his aid.

Night fell. Snow began to fall, covering everything in white. The horse was hungry and tired. When many hours had passed and no one came to take it, it picked up its feet and made its way back to the village, to the house of the coachman.

The way was already covered by snow, and the old horse went slowly. Every once in a while it stopped to rest. The horse walked along all that night. And then morning came, Friday morning.

There was nothing in the coachman's home for the Sabbath. The stove was empty. All the shelves in the pantry were bare. Everyone in the house was hungry. But the coachman went, as usual, to immerse himself in the ritual bath, and then went to the synagogue. Before he went he reminded his wife not to take anything from anyone. After he left his wife began to clean the house. Even if they had nothing for the Sabbath, at least the house would be sparkling clean. The children sat next to the empty and cold stove. They were very hungry and very sad.

And then they suddenly heard a noise in the courtyard.

"I thought I heard our horse," the youngest son said.

They all hurried outside, and look – next to the gate they found the horse, harnessed to the wagon, as if calling for help. It was half-frozen from the cold, hungry and exhausted.

"Who could have loaded so many logs on such an old and weak horse?" the wife asked angrily at the sight of the heavily-loaded wagon.

The woman and her children began unloading the branches from the wagon, so that they could put them in the cold stove.

And then – what did they see? Underneath the branches they found sacks full of gold coins. A treasure!

The little boy ran to the synagogue to tell his father the good news. But the coachman did not want to interrupt his prayers, not even for a single minute. So the coachman did not know what had happened in his house. He stayed in the synagogue all day Friday, and did not leave until all the other Jews had left. He was afraid that they might ask him why the windows of his house were dark on Sabbath eve.

Only after the Sabbath had entered, after all the other Jews in the synagogue had gone to their homes, did the coachman also leave the synagogue and go on his way. Joy and sadness

were intermingled in his heart. Joy, because he had overcome the urge to ask people for charity; sadness, because this time he had nothing with which to honor the Sabbath.

As he was walking, when he approached his house – now, what's this? A great light was shining from all the windows of his house! Where had his wife gotten the money to buy so many candles? Had she forgotten her promise, and taken charity from their neighbors?

The coachman walked into his house – straight into the Garden of Eden! The candles were burning, there was wine on the table, Sabbath *hallot*, meat, fish, and all manner of good things. The house was a palace, filled with all kinds of good smells, the special smell of the Sabbath. Where did all this come from?

His children ran to greet him. They told him everything that had happened: how the horse had brought them a treasure from the forest!

And so the poor coachman became a very rich man. He no longer had to work so hard in order to support his family. He sat and studied day and night, and became known as a great scholar. And now that he was rich, he did not forget the poor people. So that they would not be ashamed, he gave charity secretly, to everyone who was in need.

And for his faithful old horse, who had brought the treasure from the forest, he built a new, spacious barn. He gave the horse the very best food. And the horse stood in his new barn, ate and drank, and enjoyed life.

The Candle That Burned All Night

There was once a Jew who lived in a small town in Poland. His name was Shabtai, and he was a bookbinder. Shabtai was a simple poor person. He had only one son, who was named Hayim. This child was very intelligent. By the time he was seven years old, he already knew so much Torah that there was no teacher in the entire city who was capable of teaching him anything new. Hayim therefore had to go to the rabbi of the city, who was a great scholar, and he taught Hayim in his own house.

All day long the child sat in the rabbi's house and studied. And what did he do at night? At night he wanted to study by himself, in his own home. But his family was very poor, and candles burned in his house only on the Sabbath. The child could not study in the dark. Besides which, there were not many books in his father's house. There was only a prayerbook and a *humash*, the Five Books of Moses. How could the child learn without the Talmud and the other holy books of Torah?

Hayim begged his father to permit him to go in the evenings to the study hall to learn. There were many books there, and there were candles which the *shamash*, the attendant, lit for the people studying there. But how could a child go to the study hall, which was far from his home? It was dark outside and he was only a little boy.

"I'm not afraid, Father," the child insisted. "I'm not afraid of the dark."

"But I am afraid for you," his father hesitated. "You are a little child, it is a great distance, and the night is very dark."

"We're worried about your health, too," his mother added. "It isn't good for a child your age to sit late at night and study. You are liable to become sick, God forbid."

"Please, Father," the child asked," "I won't get sick, Mother."

"Perhaps I will let you go for only one hour," his father finally agreed.

"I promise you, I won't sit in the study hall more than one hour each night," Hayim said to his father.

That night Shabtai accompanied his son Hayim to the study hall. The father whispered in

the ear of the *shamash*, not to give his son more than one candle. When the candle would burn down and go out, the child would know that the time had come to return home. The *shamash* promised him that he would do this. Shabtai felt better, and went home. He knew that his son would return home at the end of the hour. Shabtai sat down to finish his work of binding books. He had to work at night as well, so that he could buy bread for his family. He sat and worked, and waited for his son.

An hour passed – but his son had still not returned home.

"Shabtai, where's Hayim?" the worried mother asked.

"He'll surely come in a little while. Why, he promised me that he would not sit there more than an hour, and the *shamash* promised me that he would not give him a second candle to study by," Shabtai said to his wife, and continued with his work.

Another hour passed, but Hayim still had not returned home.

"Shabtai, go and see what has happened to our child!" the mother asked.

Shabtai stood up from his work and said, "Hayim must have encountered a problem in his studies, one that he did not understand, and went to the rabbi to ask him. I will go to the rabbi's house and bring Hayim home." Shabtai put on his heavy coat and his hat and went out of the house. It was dark and bitterly cold outside. Snow was falling. The white flakes fell on Shabtai's face. It was silent outside. The streets were deserted. Everyone had already gone to sleep. Only Shabtai was walking through the city, in the cold and the snow, on his way to the house of the rabbi.

When he came to the rabbi's home, he saw that the house was dark, and all the shutters were drawn. Maybe the rabbi was sitting with little Hayim in one of the small inner rooms? Shabtai went up to the door and knocked softly. He did not want to awaken the members of the rabbi's family who were already asleep. He knocked again, and then a third time, until he heard a voice from within the house: "Who's there?"

"It's me, Shabtai," he whispered to the closed door.

"I'll open up immediately."

Shabtai stood in front of the locked door and waited. After a little while, which seemed to him like years, the door opened. The rabbi stood on the threshold. "Reb Shabtai! What brings you here at such an hour?" he asked, surprised.

"I'm looking for my son. Didn't he come here to you?" Shabtai asked. His heart was pounding with worry.

"Your son? No, I haven't seen him since he left after we finished studying for the day," the rabbi answered him.

"He hasn't come home.... He hasn't returned from the study hall," he said. His face was white with fear. "He promised me that he would not stay there more than an hour, and just look...."

"If he promised you, he will certainly keep his word," the rabbi said.

"But he hasn't returned home!" Shabtai repeated, "he hasn't returned...."

"Maybe it was too cold for him on the way home from the study hall, and he went into one of the warehouses, and fell asleep there," the rabbi thought. "It just isn't possible that Hayim would not keep a promise he made to his father."

The rabbi dressed in his warm clothes, put on his boots, and went out with the father to search for Hayim. Maybe he was stricken by the cold and he fell down on the road, frozen. Maybe he was attacked by night robbers who kidnapped him. These thoughts raced through the mind of the worried father. The rabbi and Shabtai walked through the streets of the city. The night's darkness was not broken by any light. The snow kept falling. The cold froze them as they walked.

They searched for hours, but could not find the child. They went to Shabtai's house – maybe the child had returned home in the meantime. But only the worried mother sat in the house. They went once again to the rabbi's house, perhaps he had taken the wrong way and arrived there by mistake. But no....

"Perhaps the tired child fell asleep on one of the benches in the study hall, when his candle went out," the rabbi raised another possibility. "How could we not have thought of that?" They walked quickly to the study hall. The night was almost over. They approached the study hall – and there was a light shining from a crack in the shutters.

Who could be sitting and studying at such an hour? It would be dawn in a little while! The two men went inside, and what did they see? A candle was burning, and little Hayim was sitting and studying. "Hayim," his father called, enraged, "you promised me!"

"You are studying the Torah, and you don't know that it is written 'Honor your father' in the Ten Commandments," the rabbi rebuked him.

The child heard the voices addressed to him, and turned his head away from the book before him. And then the candle went out, and the entire study hall was dark.

Shabtai thought that his son had blown out the candle, so that they would not see him. He became even angrier.

"Isn't it bad enough that you do not honor your father, that you don't even honor the rabbi?"

The *shamash*, who was sleeping in a side room in the study hall, heard the voices. He lit a candle and came into the study hall. The rabbi stood on one side, and Shabtai stood on the other side. The boy stood in the middle, trembling and crying.

"Ungrateful child!" Shabtai shouted, furious. "It isn't enough that you didn't keep your promise, you even ..."

"No – no -" Hayim cried, and could not say anything because of his crying.

"I don't understand," the *shamash* said, "I gave him only one candle, which would last only one hour. Where did he get more candles to last the entire night? The candles are locked away in my room, and the key is around my neck."

"I didn't take any candles. I only had the one candle. I didn't know that an hour had passed. The candle burned all the time," Hayim said through his tears.

And then the rabbi understood what had happened. "Don't be angry with your son, Reb Shabtai," he said, "now I understand everything."

"But I still don't understand anything," Shabtai said. He was very happy that he had found his son safe and sound, but he was exceedingly angry at his son's actions. Not only had he broken his promise, he had apparently taken candles that weren't his. He told stories that he had completely made up.

"Hayim did not do all these bad things," the rabbi said, as if he knew what the father was thinking. "When he began to study in the study hall at night, by himself, there was much joy in Heaven. The angels rejoiced greatly," the rabbi explained, "and when the angels rejoice, the candle in the study hall does not go out. But when we came here, we began to talk, and the child stopped studying. Then the celebrating stopped in Heaven, and the candle went out." This is what the rabbi explained to everyone in the study hall. Everyone was amazed by this. A miracle had been performed for little Hayim, a miracle from Heaven. The candle which was supposed to burn for only one hour had provided him with light for the entire night.

Shabtai took his son home, and the worried mother was very glad. And from then on Shabtai permitted his son to study as long as he wanted. Hayim sat every night in the study hall. He returned home alone, and nothing bad happened to him. And when he grew up, he became a great Torah scholar.

The Tales:

1. The Birth of the Baal Shem Tov
2. The Story of the Sorcerer Valkilak
3. The Horse Who Brought a Treasure
4. The Candle That Burned All Night